Directed Drawing II

A collection of directed drawings designed to teach the beginning artist how to draw people.

Written By: Tracy Jarboe & Stefani Sadler

Illustrated By: Stefani Sadler

Dear Teachers,

 We have worked very hard at creating this packet for you. We hope you are excited about these activities and enjoy using them in your classroom. We kindly ask that you honor the copyright of our materials and do not "freely share" this packet with all your friends and colleagues. If others like these activities as well, simply refer them to the website at which you purchased yours and they may purchase a set as well. When copyrighted materials are photocopied for, or emailed to others, this is not only breaking the law, it is just not nice. We want to continue providing materials for you at an affordable cost. Thank you for your thoughtful consideration of copyright.

Original Copyright © 2009 by Stefani Sadler and Tracy Jarboe

All rights reserved. **No** part of this book other than the specified blackline masters may be reproduced mechanically, electronically, photocopying or any other means without prior written consent, except in the case of book reviews. The specified blackline masters may only be reproduced for the purchaser's <u>individual</u> classroom use and may not be used for school-wide or district distribution without prior written permission from <u>ABC Schoolhouse</u>. Additional copies of this publication & site licenses are available online through the <u>ABC Schoolhouse</u> website. All artwork is the creation of Stefani Sadler and Each image is also under copyright.

<u>ABC Schoolhouse</u>
<u>www.abcschoolhouse.com</u>
3245 Black Canyon Road
Colorado Springs, CO 80904

Introduction

As teachers with over 20 years of experience each, we have always believed that a hands-on, creative, and balanced approach to instruction is the most successful framework for developing skills in young children. As both parents and educators we know that involving children in the arts and providing children with ample opportunity to create, while using a wide variety of media, provides a strong research-based foundation for academic development.

We have enjoyed and practiced techniques we have learned from educational leaders such as Mona Brookes and Betty Edwards. However, with a movement in recent years to teach to standardized tests, many teachers have felt pressured to stop providing the opportunity to explore the arts. We know that research has shown time and time again, the importance of art in the educational process. Children who are exposed to music and art instruction do much better in reading, math and science. They develop a greater curiosity about, understanding of, and appreciation for the subject matter being taught. We know that providing arts in education stimulates better behavior, personal esteem, and socialization skills. So why do so many educators discount it's importance and so many children stop drawing by second grade? The truth is that whole learning is a combination of current research, sound philosophy, balanced curriculum, and good teaching practice!

For many years we have been teaching, presenting, and publishing materials that integrate music, art, movement, and literature across the curriculum. Even though we now have a wealth of quality materials and training available to us, as teachers we are always learning and modifying our educational practice and supplementing district adopted curriculum. The activities in this book are not intended to replace core instruction, but rather to enhance and extend the concepts taught within this practice. Many of these patterns may be used as independent practice and are applicable to both school and home learning.

We sincerely hope you will find these activities and drawing patterns complimentary to your instructional program and that the children you teach will find joy and success in reading, writing and drawing!

Drawing People

Beyond the step-by-step examples found in this e-book, we have provided a "feature gallery." This gallery offers numerous variations for hair, eyes, noses, and so on. You may wish to enlarge and post these at your center or even give each student their own desk copy for reference. Be sure to laminate the gallery page or place it inside a page protector. This process will allow you to use the page over and over again.

Please remember that when learning a new skill your students may feel slightly intimidated and unsure of their abilities. It is vital to offer praise and encouragement throughout the process. This will not only allow the students to feel safe and willing to take risks, but will result in greater confidence and ability. We also encourage you to make mistakes in front of the students and take that opportunity to share that true learning is found in the process and not necessarily the product.

Learning to draw a self-portrait is a valuable exercise and a fun beginning activity as young students tend to be egocentric and enjoy learning, sharing, and drawing themselves. It's helpful to provide students with mirrors so that they can spend time studying their features before transferring them to paper. Many science curriculum kits come with mirrors and if your grade level kit does not contain mirrors, ask another grade level if you may borrow theirs.

Another portrait experience to consider is creating buddy portraits. Place the students in groups of two or in "buddies". Then ask each student to study the features of their buddy. Expect giggles and embarrassment at first, but this will quickly pass and the students will begin to seriously look at each other's hair style and texture, eye shape and color, and so on. These first portrait drawings help to ease students as they begin the drawing process and develop confidence.

Drawing People (cont.)

The concept of drawing people may be daunting and many young artists embrace the stick figure and never move beyond this concept. There are some simple techniques that help students transition from traditional stick figures to more substantial and dimensional drawings of people. This book presents these basic figure drawing techniques in a step-by-step manner. We find this method works well in both an independent center and in a teacher-directed drawing lesson that is completed on a white board, chart paper, overhead projector, or docu-cam.

Perfection of product is not the objective of this book, but rather the opportunity to practice and develop drawing skills, fine-motor control, listening skills, visual-spatial thinking, and analysis through patient and kind teacher direction. The exercises in this book may be repeated periodically, allowing the process to become natural and automatic. Drawings may also be completed in color and we do encourage you to explore the use of varied media including: colored pencil, chalk, or crayon. As the students gain ability and confidence they may begin to create more of a composition using one or more figures. Thematic figures that you may find helpful while teaching specific themes have also been provided in this book. Remember to offer continual praise and encouragement as we feel practice + praise = successful performance.

How to Use This Book

We have found that directed drawing is best taught using the following approach:

1. First read aloud a quality piece of literature to entice student interest and promote learning. We have provided a selection of literature titles to get you started.

2. Model and discuss the process for students by drawing each figure in a step-by-step manner with the children. After having experienced drawing figures several times as a class and the process has been learned, new figure drawings may then be completed independently by following the simple step-by-step pictorial directions provided. Photocopy these step-by-step pictorial directions onto cardstock and then laminate each to create directed drawing cards. We have used directed drawing cards successfully during independent center time.

4. Extend the learning process by incorporating different forms of media in the completion of each art piece. Students may color, paint, and embellish their drawings. We have listed several ideas for you to consider besides coloring the drawing with crayons. You may choose to try one of these alternatives to provide additional art experiences.

5. It is important to provide opportunities for students to revisit the drawing process independently in follow-up activities such as a writing extension. We have provided four drawing frames to choose from and three of these have space provided for writing extensions.

Table of Contents

We have included several directed drawings in this "people" themed volume. These drawings have been specifically designed for beginning artists. Even the youngest children will experience success with these drawings. If you desire a greater challenge, you may consider adding more detail to each of the drawings.

1. Young Boy I
2. Young Boy II
3. Young Girl I
4. Young Girl II
5. Woman
6. Man
7. Older Woman
8. Older Man
9. Infant
10. Positions
11. Features
12. Hats
13. Pirate
14. Cowboy
15. Clown
16. Princess
17. Pilgrim Boy
18. Pilgrim Girl
19. Indian Boy
20. Indian Girl
21. Book Cover

Extensions for Figure Drawings

Literature Suggestions

1. *What I Like About Me* by Allia Zobel Nolan and Miki Sakamoto
2. *I Like Me* by Nancy Carlson
3. *I Like Myself* by Karen Beaumont and David Catrow
4. *I'm Gonna Like Me* and/or *Is There Really a Human Race?* by Jamie Lee Curtis and Laura Cornell
5. *Whoever You Are* by Mem Fox
6. *People* by Peter Spier
7. *Just Like Me: Stories & Self-Portraits by Fourteen Artists* by Harriet Rohmer
8. *David's Drawings* by Cathryn Falwell
9. *Will I Have a Friend?* By Miriam Cohen
10. *100 is a Family* by Pam Ryan
11. *A Rainbow of Friends* by P. K. Hallinan
12. *Drawing Lessons From a Bear* by David McPhail

This list of books has been provided as a helpful reference. The illustrations styles are all very different and many of the books promote discussion that would help in the figure drawing process. We encourage you to discuss the illustrations in any picture book you read. This process allows students to see that each of us has our own unique drawing style and that figure drawings do not have to look like photographs. Some of the figures are realistic, but others are abstract, cute, or cartoon like. Taking the time to discuss how each artist interprets figure drawing differently, will allow your students the freedom to express their own unique style.

Writing Extension

Pages containing a drawing frame and writing area have been provided in order to allow you to incorporate writing activities into the art process. For example, if you are going to do a buddy drawing activity you may choose to read a friendship book first, then draw buddies and finally write about your buddy. What makes this buddy a good friend? What are some of his/her likes or dislikes, talents, hobbies, and so on. The possibilities to integrate drawing across the curriculum are vast and we encourage you to integrate curriculum as often as possible.

- You will find the drawing and drawing/writing frames on the following four pages.

Art Tips

1. Use chalk pastels to color the drawing. The chalk colors may be easily blended using a cotton ball or Q-tip. They will give the picture a light, fluffy appearance. It is worth investing in quality chalk. They will last a long time and perform much better.
2. The use of watercolor paints may also give that soft, smooth appearance. Be sure the paints are well-diluted with water before applying to the paper.

Advanced Drawings

Once the students have become familiar with the figure drawing process they will be ready to attempt more advanced characters. We have provided eight advanced characters that your students may wish to sketch. Remind students that they are always able to refer back to the reference pages showing positions, features, and hats for assistance.

Remember to focus on the process, not the product, and have fun!

By:

By:

Name:

Name:

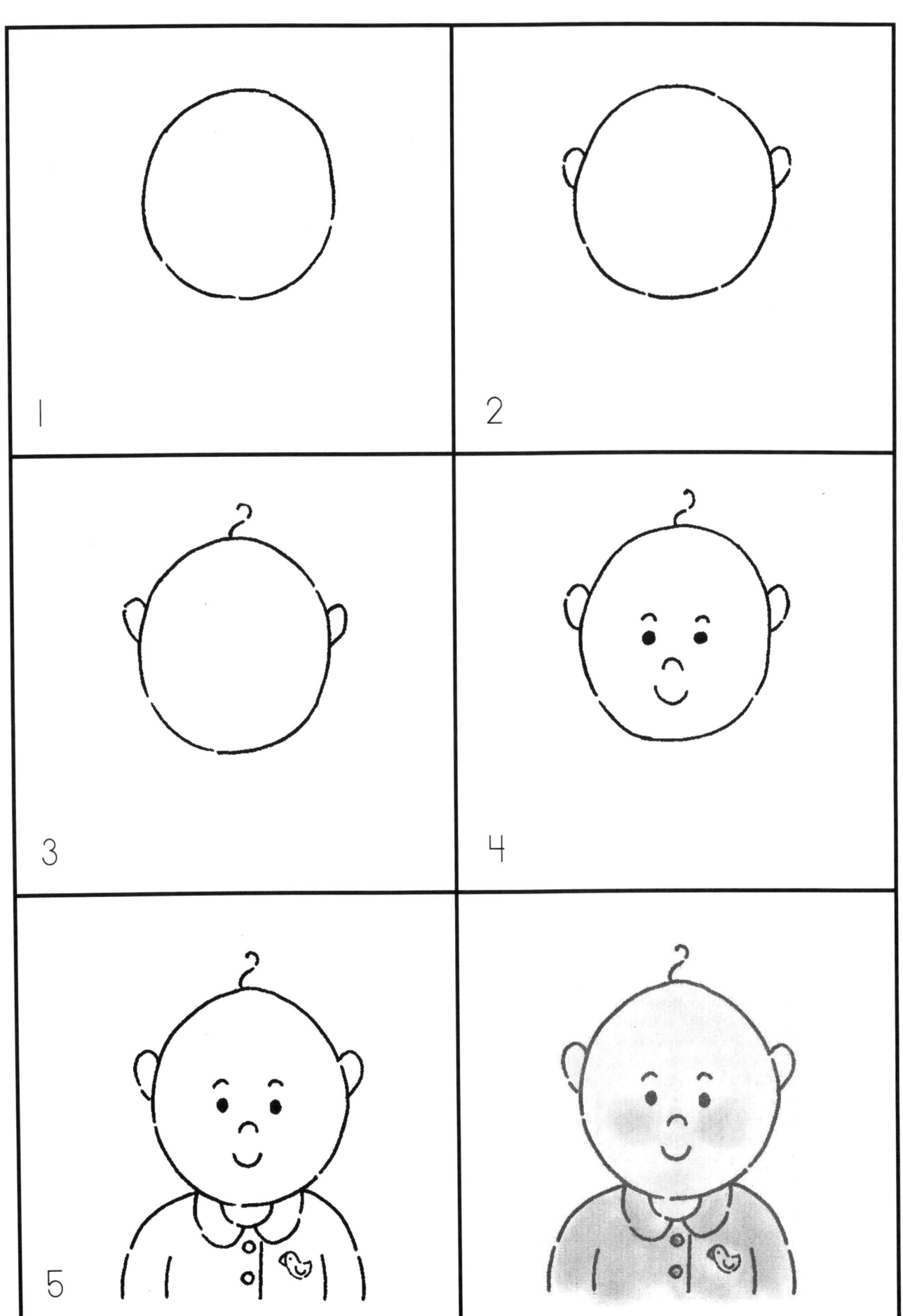

Standing Figure

Sitting Figure

Walking Figure

Running Figure

Features

Expressions

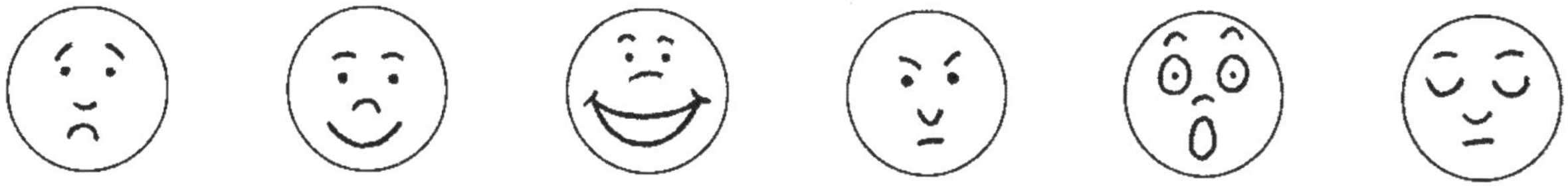

Noses

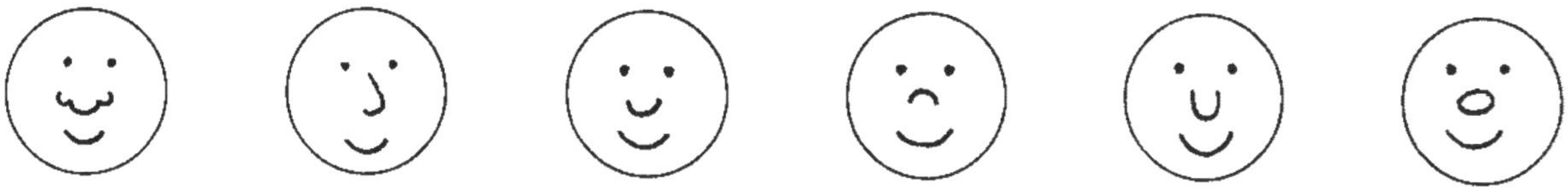

Eyes

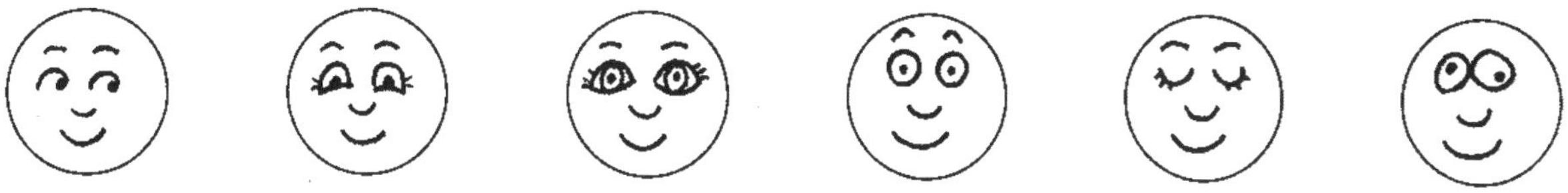

Mouths

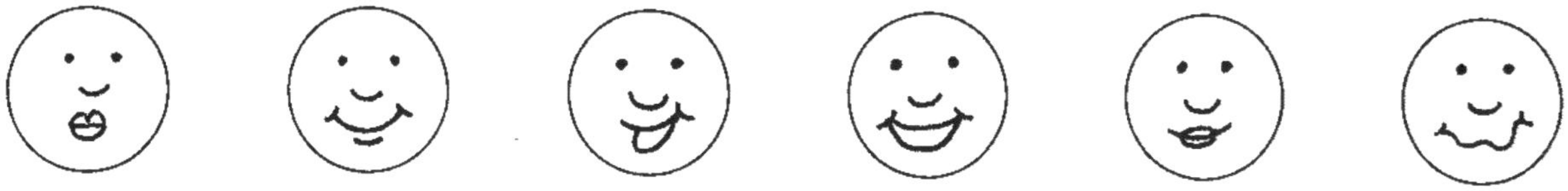

Hair

Hair

Hats are a quick and easy way to give a figure character and personality. Practice with placement of the hat and what will work the best for your drawing. Bringing in a selection of hats for the Art Center or sketching times is very helpful.

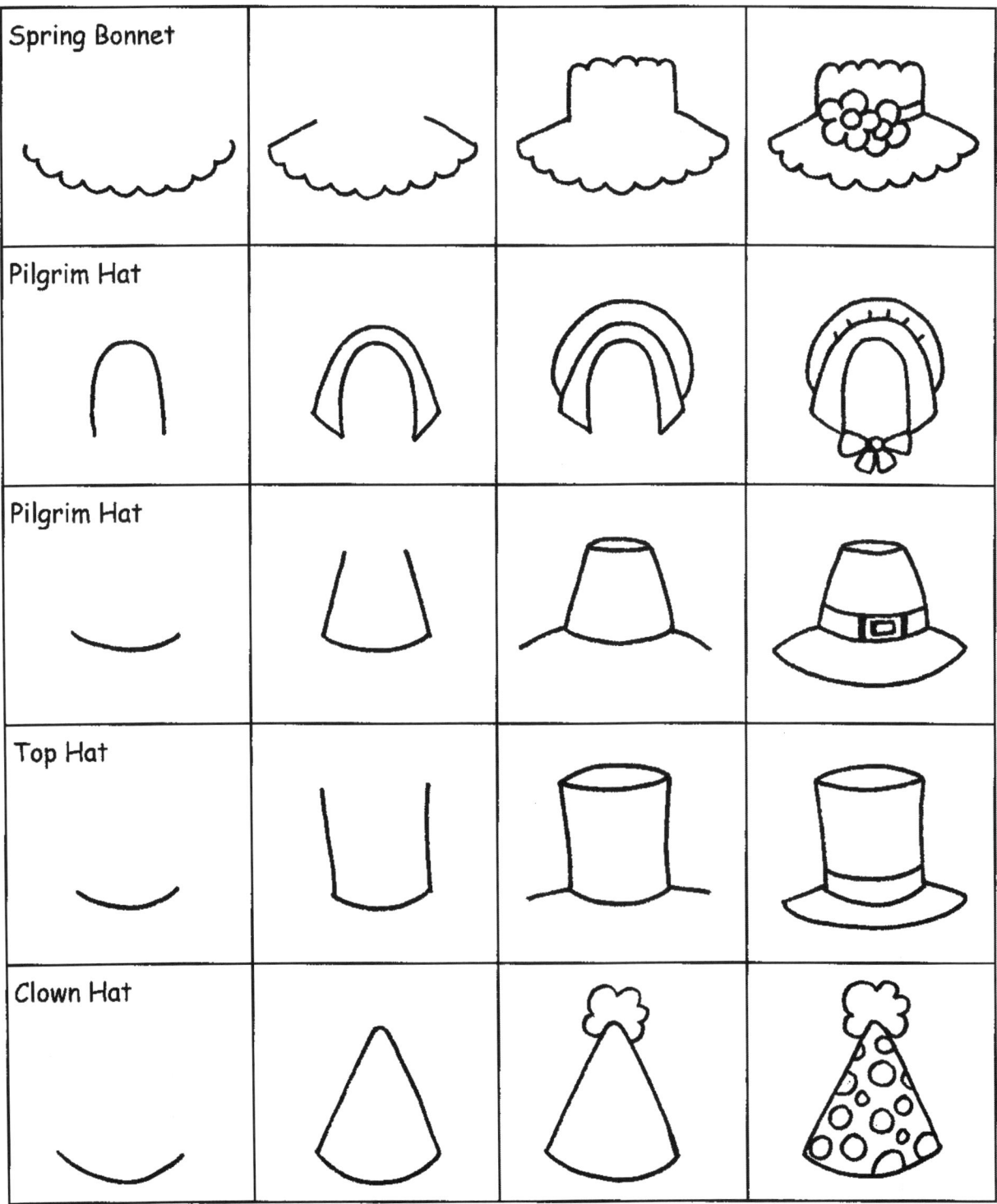

Santa Hat			
Chef Hat			
Cowboy Hat			
Pirate Hat			
Sailor Hat			
Sombrero			

Baby Bonnet			
Crown			
Police Officer			
Stocking Cap			
Witch Hat			
Helmet			

Straw Hat			
Rain Hat			
Leprechaun Hat			
Baseball Cap			
Fire Hat			
Beanie			

Advanced Figures - Pirate

Advanced Figures - Cowboy

Advanced Figures - Clown

Advanced Figures - Princess

Advanced Figures - Pilgrim Boy

Advanced Figures - Pilgrim Girl

Advanced Figures - Indian Boy

Advanced Figures - Indian Girl

My Book of Drawings

By: _____

Printed in Great Britain
by Amazon.co.uk, Ltd.,
Marston Gate.